W9-AUK-324

SCIENCE 808
Machines 2

LIFEPAC Test is located in the center of the booklet. Please remove before starting the unit.

Authors:
Shirley A. Johnson, M.N.S.
Virginia Mountain

Editor-in-Chief:
Richard W. Wheeler, M.A.Ed.
Editor:
Lee H. Dunning, M.S.T., M.S.Ed.
Consulting Editor:
Harold Wengert, Ed.D.
Revision Editor:
Alan Christopherson, M.S.

Westover Studios Design Team:
Phillip Pettet, Creative Lead
Teresa Davis, DTP Lead
Nick Castro
Andi Graham
Jerry Wingo
Don Lechner

Alpha Omega
PUBLICATIONS

804 N. 2nd Ave. E.
Rock Rapids, IA 51246-1759

© MCMXCVI by Alpha Omega Publications, Inc. All rights reserved.
LIFEPAC is a registered trademark of Alpha Omega Publications, Inc.

All trademarks and/or service marks referenced in this material are the property of their respective owners. Alpha Omega Publications, Inc. makes no claim of ownership to any trademarks and/or service marks other than their own and their affiliates, and makes no claim of affiliation to any companies whose trademarks may be listed in this material, other than their own.

Machines 2

Introduction

The use of tools is mentioned throughout the Bible. Noah used tools to build the ark that saved mankind from the flood waters. Tools have helped mankind build altars and temples to worship the Lord. God has given human beings the skills to develop and use tools. Tools are simple machines. In this LIFEPAC® you will study six simple machines and how humans use them.

The development of machines encouraged mankind to build, to invent, to travel, and to work. People can do more work with machines than they can without.

Machines are not as useful as they might be because friction makes them less efficient. Friction causes them to wear out, to slow down, and to stop. The work that mankind was designed to do is slowed down by the friction of bad relationships between people.

Objectives

Read these objectives. The objectives tell you what you will be able to do when you have successfully completed this LIFEPAC. When you have finished this LIFEPAC, you should be able to:

1. Define friction and describe its effects.

2. Identify three kinds of friction.

3. Name three ways to reduce friction.

4. Calculate the coefficient of friction.

5. Identify three classes of levers.

6. Define and calculate the mechanical advantage and efficiency of a lever.

7. List the uses of the wheel and axle, pulley, and gears.

8. Calculate the mechanical advantage of the wheel and axle and pulleys.

9. Identify the uses of the inclined plane, wedge, and screw.

10. Calculate the mechanical advantage of the inclined plane, wedge, and screw.

Survey the LIFEPAC. Ask yourself some questions about this study and write your questions here.

1. FRICTION

In the winter when the sidewalks are covered with snow and ice, we sand them to increase the **friction** between the steps and our feet. We apply oil to engines and motors to reduce the friction between moving parts.

Without friction even walking would be impossible; but friction causes engines to wear out. Friction is both helpful and harmful. In this section you will study the forces of friction, the types of friction, and some ways to reduce friction.

SECTION OBJECTIVES

Review these objectives. When you have completed this section, you should be able to:

1. Define friction and describe its effects.
2. Identify three kinds of friction.
3. Name three ways to reduce friction.
4. Calculate the coefficient of friction.

VOCABULARY

Study these words to enhance your learning success in this section.

coefficient (kō u fish' unt). A ratio used to calculate the value of a quantity under different conditions.

fluid (flü' id). Any substance, liquid or gas, that flows.

force (fôrs). A push or a pull.

friction (frik' shun). The force that resists moving one object against another.

lubricant (lü' bru kunt). Substance used to make an object slippery or smooth; commonly, oil or grease.

normal force (nôr' mul fôrs). The force that is perpendicular to the surface between two objects; the attraction of gravity for an object on a level surface.

Note: *All vocabulary words in this LIFEPAC appear in* **boldface** *print the first time they are used. If you are not sure of the meaning when you are reading, study the definitions given.*

Pronunciation Key: hat, āge, cãre, fär; let, ēqual, tėrm; it, īce; hot, ōpen, ôrder; oil; out; cup, pu̇t, rüle; child; long; thin; /ŦH/ for then; /zh/ for measure; /u/ or /ə/ represents /a/ in about, /e/ in taken, /i/ in pencil, /o/ in lemon, and /u/ in circus.

FORCES OF FRICTION

Many factors, including **friction**, slope, and material, act to change the speed of an object. For centuries people tried to invent perpetual-motion machines. Perpetual-motion machines would create their own energy and never stop working. People have not been able to invent such a machine. Friction is the **force** that always stopped them. You will study the force of friction in this section.

Definition. Friction is a force that resists motion. It occurs when a surface in motion rubs against another surface. Friction acts parallel to the surfaces that are moving against (contacting) one another and in the direction opposite to the direction of motion. Friction resists (opposes) motion.

If you put a box on the sidewalk and push it, the box moves. You have exerted a force. Friction will cause the box to stop moving after traveling a short distance. A resisting force has acted. The box will not move again unless you give it another push.

Friction is present whenever motion occurs. Car engines are designed to produce as little friction as possible. Narrow-wheeled bicycles offer less resistance to friction than other bicycles.

Causes. Friction is caused by rough surfaces rubbing together as objects move over each other. Surfaces are polished to lessen friction as much as possible. Engineers design shapes to lessen air resistance. When two very highly polished surfaces are together, the friction between them *increases*. The explanation proposed is that atomic bonding, of a sort, exists between the two surfaces.

Uses. Friction makes walking possible. The friction between shoe and floor increases with roughness. Walking becomes easier. Imagine walking on polished ice with waxed shoes!

Vehicles use friction to slow down and stop. Brakes depend upon friction. The resistance between tire and road slows cars and trucks. Tires are designed with a tread to increase friction. Wet roads are more dangerous than dry roads because water lessens the tires' friction on the road surface. Tires are tested on wet roads to determine stopping distance and skid resistance.

Without friction any little force you exerted on an object would send you in one direction and would send the object in the opposite direction. This example illustrates Newton's Law: Every force has an equal and opposite force. In space, friction with air does not exist. When astronauts push on a spaceship, it moves one way and they move another.

Write the letter of the correct choice.

1.1 Tires are designed to _____ .
   a. increase friction   b. decrease friction   c. have no relation to friction

1.2 *Very* smooth surfaces _____ .
   a. have little or no friction   b. do not need friction to move
   c. have increased friction

✎ **Complete these sentences.**

1.3 Motion is always accompanied by _____ .

1.4 Friction acts _____ (parallel, perpendicular) to surfaces in contact.

Complete these activities.

For each item write *D* if it is a desirable type of friction or write *U* if it is an undesirable type of friction.

1.5 _____ friction between road and tires

1.6 _____ friction between parts of an engine

1.7 _____ friction between your shoes and the floor

1.8 _____ no friction at all

TYPES OF FRICTION

Friction forces apply mostly to solids. Gases and liquids offer resistance to motion, but they are difficult to measure and study in the classroom or laboratory. Comparison of different frictional forces is possible in the laboratory: The force needed to keep an object moving can be measured with a scale. If you pull an object with a spring scale, you find that the object requires more force to start moving than to keep moving. This force that opposes the start of motion is referred to as *starting friction*.

Sliding. *Sliding* friction is resistance to motion after the object has begun to move. Sliding friction is dependent on the materials that make up the surfaces in contact.

In the past, farmers removed rocks from their fields by loading them on a horse-drawn flatbed. The horses worked, and the wooden flatbed dragged against the ground.

Sliding friction is affected very little by the speed or the surface area of the moving object. It *is* affected by the force that presses the surfaces together. This force is called the **normal force**. On level surfaces the normal force is the weight of the object.

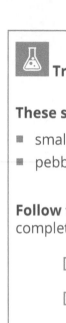 **Try this investigation.**

These supplies are needed:

- small match box
- pebbles
- coins (pennies are best)
- string (about 24 inches long)
- small plastic bag

Follow these directions and complete the sentence. Put a check in the box when each step is completed.

☐ 1. Fill the match box with pebbles.

☐ 2. Tie the string to the box. Allow the string to hang over the edge of the table.

☐ 3. Tie this end of the string to the plastic bag, leaving an opening to put in coins.

☐ 4. Add coins one by one until the box is pulled off the table.

☐ 5. Count and record the number of coins.

1.9   The number of coins needed to pull the box off the table was

_____ .

 Do not put this activity away; you will be using it again.

Force of Friction Experiment

Rolling. Early in history most cultures discovered that rolling objects was easier than dragging them. To move a flat object, a cylindrical roller was placed beneath it. The object could then be rolled over the ground. The first rollers were probably logs. The logs had to be carried around to the front of the object after the object had passed over them. This method still involved hard work, but it was easier than dragging the object. The friction involved in sliding an object is great; rolling friction is much less.

Roller bearings and steel rollers are used to reduce friction in moving small and large objects. House movers use steel rollers to position buildings. Ball bearings permit low friction motion in all directions and are used to reduce friction in automobile wheels, bicycle wheels, and machines.

Try this investigation.

These supplies are needed:

- all items from previous investigation
- 8 or 10 round sticks (pencils, Tinker Toys, dowels)

Follow these directions and answer the questions. Put a check in the box when each step is completed.

☐ 1. Lay the round sticks on the table about 1 inch apart and about 2 inches back from the edge of the table.

☐ 2. Put the match box from Activity 1.9 on the rollers farthest away from the edge.

☐ 3. Now add coins one by one to the bag until the box is pulled off the table.

☐ 4. Count and record the number of coins.

1.10 How many coins were needed to pull the box off the table? _____

1.11 Is this number less than in 1.9? _____

1.12 What is your explanation for 1.11? _____

_____

_____

Overcoming Friction Experiment

Fluid. Gases and liquids also offer resistance to motion. Air resists the motion of cars and airplanes. These vehicles are designed to offer the least possible *air resistance*. Boats must overcome the resistance of the water, and they have hulls shaped to lessen resistance to motion. Frictions that involve liquids and gases are examples of **fluid** friction.

We streamline cars and airplanes to reduce fluid friction. Even the rivets on an airplane increase the friction. The surfaces are as smooth as the builder can make them to reduce the friction between the airplane and the air.

Write true or false.

1.13 _____ Streamlining a car or boat can increase speed by decreasing friction.

1.14 _____ Gases and fluids do not produce friction.

1.15 _____ Sliding friction is affected by the weight of the object.

1.16 _____ Smooth surfaces can decrease fluid friction.

Complete these sentences.

1.17 The force needed to start an object in motion is increased by _____ friction.

1.18 The motion of an object being pulled over a surface is called _____ friction.

1.19 Ball bearings are an example of _____ friction.

1.20 The resistance of air to a moving object is called _____ friction.

 Try one of these investigations.

1.21 Select and complete *one* of the following activities.

A. Go to the library and look at pictures of early automobiles. Compare them with the shape of present cars. Describe the differences and tell how friction may have helped to change the shape of cars.

B. Make a drawing of a car, boat, or plane that you think would offer the least resistance to fluid friction. Your drawing should be on plain white paper, 8½ x 11 in size.

C. Make a list of places in your home that friction may occur. You should have at least ten items. After each item tell if it is sliding, rolling, or fluid friction taking place.

TEACHER CHECK _____ _____
initials   date

REDUCING FRICTION

In certain situations friction is necessary, but in other instances we wish to eliminate as much friction as possible. Many methods and combinations of methods can be used to lessen the effects of friction.

Lubrication. Years ago the wagons used to haul grain to market had wooden wheels and axles. They were heavily loaded and gave off a piercing noise as they moved across the prairie. The noise was lessened when a **lubricant**, grease, was applied to reduce the friction between the wheel and axle.

Lubrication with oil, grease, or other lubricants lessens the friction. Petroleum products have molecules that slide on each other with little resistance. Graphite is carbon with flat crystals. These crystals slide over each other easily. Graphite is a lubricant that has many specialized uses. Because it is a powder, graphite can be blown into locks to lubricate the mechanism.

Shapes. The *shape* of an object determines how much resistance it will receive as it moves over a surface. Shapes that roll across a surface, like rollers or ball bearings, have the least resistance. Aircraft, automobiles, boats, and submarines have sleek, tapering lines to permit fluids to flow over them with the least resistance.

If you try to move a variety of shapes through water, you can estimate the effectiveness of the shape by the amount of disturbance in the water. The greater the disturbance, the greater the friction.

Friction-reducing materials. *Teflon* is a substance used to coat bearings and other parts of machines when eliminating friction is important. Teflon also coats cooking utensils to eliminate sticking. Some metallic alloys reduce friction more than other alloys. A surface of lead and antimony lessens friction when used with steel. The ratio between the force of friction and the perpendicular force is called the **coefficient** of friction.

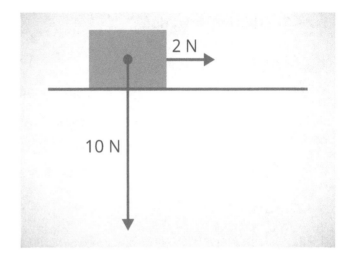

A box weighing 10 pounds (newton) is pulled along the floor by a force of 2 pounds. What is the coefficient of friction between the floor and the box? The force pressing the surfaces together is 10 lbs. (F_n); the force required to move the box is 2 lbs. (F_f). Coefficient of friction μ (the Greek letter *mu*) is

$$\mu = \frac{F_f}{F_n} = \frac{2}{10} = 0.2$$

The coefficient of friction permits a comparison of the sliding friction of different materials.

In the preceding example, the unit of force was given as the *pound*. You know that the pound is the unit of weight, so the question comes up, "Is weight a force?" The answer is "yes" because weight results from the pull—the gravitational force—that the earth exerts on objects.

The metric system (correctly called SI) unit of force (and therefore of weight) is the *newton* (N). The newton is derived from the SI base units of length (meter), time (second), and mass (kilogram). We therefore are correct in saying that an object weighs, or exerts a force of 10 newtons (10 N).

Try this investigation.

These supplies are needed:

- 2 blocks of wood
- bar of soap

Follow these directions and answer the question. Put a check in the box when each step is completed.

☐ 1. Slide the two blocks of wood over each other.

☐ 2. Then rub soap over the surface of each block and rub together again.

1.22 When were the wood blocks the easiest to rub together? _____

_____

You can use this method of lubrication to keep drawers from sticking. Safety pins or straight pins that have been stuck in a bar of soap will go through fabric much easier.

Friction-Reducing Experiment

Complete these sentences.

1.23 The use of oil or grease to lessen friction is called _____ .

1.24 To lessen friction, an airplane has a streamlined _____ .

1.25 Lead and antimony can be used to coat steel to lessen _____ .

Complete these activities.

1.26 A swimmer is going to swim across the English Channel. Before entering the water, he covers his head with a smooth plastic cap. Then he covers his body with thick grease. Explain why you think these two preparations will help him while swimming.

_____

_____

_____

1.27 A can weighing 18 newtons requires a force of 9 newtons to drag it. Calculate the coefficient of friction.

↺ **Review the material in this section in preparation for the Self Test.** The Self Test will check your mastery of this particular section. The items missed on this Self Test will indicate specific areas where restudy is needed for mastery.

SELF TEST 1

Write true or false (each answer, 1 point).

1.01 _____ Friction and motion occur at the same time.

1.02 _____ Graphite crystals can be used as a lubricant.

1.03 _____ In space fluid friction does not exist.

1.04 _____ Sliding friction occurs when an object is pulled over a surface.

1.05 _____ Teflon is used only to prevent sticking in cooking utensils.

1.06 _____ Friction should always be reduced if possible.

1.07 _____ A fluid may be either liquid or gas.

Write the letter of the correct choice (each answer, 2 points).

1.08 The shape that has the least friction in air is _____ .
a. round   b. streamlined   c. square   d. oblong

1.09 To reduce friction in a roller skate wheel, we could use _____ .
a. polished surfaces   b. ball bearings
c. a lubricant   d. a, b, and c

Complete these activities (each answer, 3 points).

1.010 Give three examples of desirable friction.

a. _____

b. _____

c. _____

1.011 Explain why friction is sometimes undesirable.

_____

_____

_____

1.012 Give three ways friction can be reduced.

a. _____

b. _____

c. _____

Describe each of these kinds of friction and give an example of where they may occur (each answer, 3 points).

1.013 sliding friction

a. description _____

b. example _____

1.014 rolling friction

a. description _____

b. example _____

1.015 fluid friction

a. description _____

b. example _____

Complete these calculations (each answer, 3 points).

1.016 A box weighing 18 newtons require a force of 6 newtons to drag it.

a. What is the coefficient of friction?

The box is coated with Teflon and now requires a force of 3 newtons to drag it.

b. What is its new coefficient of friction?

49/61   SCORE _____   TEACHER _____ _____

initials   date

2. LEVERS

When you hammer a nail, pry up a rock, or swing a baseball bat you are using a **lever**. In each instance you are using a machine to provide a force greater than the force you are exerting. We can figure the advantage of using a lever once we understand how the machine works.

Men have been using levers as machines since before the birth of Christ. Long ago the Greek scientist Archimedes described the usefulness of a lever when he said, "Give me a place to stand, and I will move the world."

SECTION OBJECTIVES

Review these objectives. When you have completed this section, you should be able to:

5. Identify three classes of levers.
6. Define and calculate the mechanical advantage and efficiency of a lever.

VOCABULARY

Study these words to enhance your learning success in this section.

actual mechanical advantage (AMA) (ak' chǔ ul mu kan' u kul ad van' tij). The ratio between the resistance force and the effort force of a machine.

efficiency (u fish' un sē). The ratio of output work to input work or the ratio of actual mechanical advantage to ideal mechanical advantage; the ability to produce the effect wanted without waste of energy.

fulcrum (ful' krum). The support on which a lever turns.

ideal mechanical advantage (IMA) (ī dē' ul ma kan' u kul ad van' tij). The ratio of the distance that the effort force moves to the distance that the resistance force moves.

lever (lev' ur). A bar that turns on a fixed point.

ratio (rā' shē ō). Relative size; quotient.

torque (tôrk). A force causing rotation; the product of a force and its perpendicular distance from a fulcrum.

MECHANICAL ADVANTAGE

We use machines to increase the effort we put into doing a job. A machine cannot multiply work. In fact, work is lost because of friction. Machines are used to do only three things. One, machines can change the size of the force. Two, machines can change the direction of the force. Three, machines can change the speed of the force.

Actual. The **actual mechanical advantage (AMA)** is a **ratio** of the weight of the object listed (the *resistance*) to the force that is exerted (the *effort*). If a long bar is used to lift a 500 lb. weight with a 20 lb. effort, the AMA is found by dividing 500 lbs. by 20 lbs. In this case, the AMA is 25. Every pound you exert produces 25 pounds on the resistance.

$$\text{AMA} = \frac{\text{weight of object}}{\text{force exerted}}$$
$$= \frac{F_r}{F_e}$$

Ideal. The **ideal mechanical advantage (IMA)** is the ratio of the distance the effort is applied to the distance the resistance is moved. If you are using a machine to move a box 2 meters and you must move your effort 4 meters, the IMA is found by dividing 4 meters by 2 meters, giving an IMA of 2. The IMA is always larger than the AMA of the same machine because IMA does not consider friction. Both IMA and AMA are pure numbers; that is, they have no units.

$$\text{IMA} = \frac{\text{distance effort applied}}{\text{distance reistance moved}}$$
$$= \frac{d_e}{d_r}$$

Activity and observation.

These supplies are needed:

- ruler
- two coins
- tape

Follow these directions and answer the question. Put a check in the box when each step is completed.

☐ 1. Place the ruler on your forefinger with the numbers in a position where you can read them. Balance the ruler and record the inch number that is over your finger. _____

☐ 2. Tape a coin on one end of the ruler.

☐ 3. Balance the ruler again and record the inch number over your finger. _____

☐ 4. Add another coin to the same end of the ruler. Balance and record the number. _____

2.1 Is your finger getting closer to the coins or farther away? _____ This activity shows how two people of unequal weight can seesaw by changing their positions.

Lever Experiment

Work. Recall that *work* is the product of a *force* times the *distance* through which the force acts. *Work input* is the product of the effort (force) and the effort distance. *Work output* is the product of the resistance (force) and the resistance distance. For example, a worker pushes down (effort) on one end of a crowbar to raise a boulder (resistance). If he is careful with his **lever** and **fulcrum**, he will make sure that his end of the bar moves farther (effort distance) than the other end moves (resistance distance).

Machines designed to multiply the effort force must apply that force through a greater distance. Because of friction, machines that merely change the direction of a force require an effort that is greater than the resistance. Work output can never be greater than work input. In actual use the work output is always less than work input.

A laboratory balance is a lever. The unknown mass (resistance) is on one side, the set of known masses (effort) is on the other. The work

| Laboratory Balance

input is adjustable because some part of the effort force, the rider, may be moved toward or away from the fulcrum.

Laboratory balances do not measure force (weight); they measure *mass*. To calculate force (weight) when mass is given in kilograms, multiply mass by 9.8 m/sec². The product will be force (weight) measured in newtons. For example, a 2 kg *mass* weighs 2 kg x 9.8 m/sec² = 19.6 N or 19.6 newtons.

Remember that the unit of force in the metric system is the *newton*.

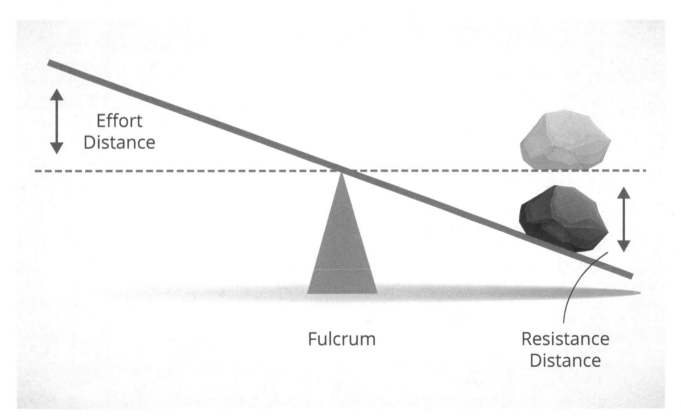

| Effort Distance and Resistance Distance of a Lever

Complete this activity.

2.2 An equal-arm balance has four kilograms on one arm.

a. What is the mass necessary to balance the arms? _____

b. Calculate this mass in newtons. _____

Efficiency. Several factors will reduce the effectiveness (the **efficiency**) of a lever. The bar might bend or the fulcrum's friction might absorb some of the effort, or the resistance might also involve friction. The efficiency of a machine can be found by dividing the work output by the work input.

$$\% \text{ efficiency} = \frac{\text{work output}}{\text{work input}} \times 100\%$$

or

$$\% \text{ efficiency} = \frac{\text{resistance} \times \text{resistance distance}}{\text{effort} \times \text{effort distance}} \times 100\%$$

Because work output is always less than work input, efficiency is always less than 100 percent.

Study this example: A board is used as a lever. The effort, a force of 520 N, moves 4 meters. The resistance, a force of 2,000 N, moves 1 meter. The efficiency is 2,000 newtons x 1 meter (work output) divided by 520 newtons x 4 meters (work input).

$$\% \text{ efficiency} = \frac{2,000 \text{ N} \times 1 \text{ m}}{520 \text{ N} \times 4 \text{ m}} \times 100\%$$

$$= \frac{2,000}{2,080} \times 100\% = 96\%$$

Efficiency may be found also by dividing the AMA by the IMA.

$$\% \text{ efficiency} = \frac{\text{AMA}}{\text{IMA}} \times 100\%$$

$$= \frac{\frac{\text{reistance force}}{\text{effort force}}}{\frac{\text{effort distance}}{\text{reistance distance}}} \times 100\%$$

$$\% \text{ efficiency} = \frac{\frac{2,000 \text{ N}}{520 \text{ N}}}{\frac{4 \text{ m}}{1 \text{ m}}} \times 100\% = 96\%$$

The compound numerator is the AMA; the compound denominator, the IMA.

Consider a lever that uses an effort force of 65 newtons to move a resistance of 100 newtons. The effort moves 4 meters and the resistance moves 2 meters. What are the IMA, AMA, and the efficiency?

a. IMA $= \dfrac{4 \text{ m}}{2 \text{ m}} = 2$

b. AMA $= \dfrac{100 \text{ N}}{65 \text{ N}} = 1.54$

c. % efficiency $= \dfrac{1.54}{2} \times 100\% = 77\%$

The efficiency of a lever varies with the type and structure of the lever. The skill of the user also enters into the efficiency. A lever balanced on a knife-edged fulcrum is very efficient. An equal-arm balance is almost 100 percent efficient.

If 2 kilograms are on one arm of an equal-arm balance, what mass of corn on the other arm would balance the arms?

■ Answer: 2 kilograms

What would be the weight of the corn?

■ Answer: 2 kilograms x 9.8 m/sec² = 19.6 newtons.

Complete this activity.

2.3 A lever is nine meters long. A load is placed at one end, three meters from the fulcrum. The load is 6,000 newtons. The effort force of 4,000 newtons is six meters from the fulcrum.

a. Calculate the IMA.

b. Calculate the AMA.

c. Calculate the efficiency (in %).

Torque. A relationship exists between the distance through which a force moves and the distance from the force to the fulcrum. Intuitively obvious to the most casual observer is the fact that a longer lever would allow for a longer effort distance; a shorter lever, a shorter effort distance. The product of a force and its distance to the fulcrum is called **torque**. A lever has clockwise torque and counterclockwise torque, determined by the direction the lever would spin if allowed to do so. A torque to the left turns a lever in a counterclockwise direction. A torque to the right turns the lever clockwise. When a lever is balanced, the torque to the left equals the torque to the right.

The torques can be balanced by equating the product of the distance and the force for each arm. Study this example: If a force of one newton acts at the end of a 0.3 meter arm of a 0.8 meter lever, what force at the end of the 0.5 meter arm will balance the lever?

0.3 meters × 1 newton = 0.5 meters × ?

$$? = \frac{0.3 \text{ meters} \times 1 \text{ newton}}{0.5 \text{ meters}} = 0.6 \text{ newtons}$$

Both torque and work are products of force and distance. Work is the product of a force and a distance that have the same direction. Torque is the product of a force and a distance at right angles to each other.

To further examine this relationship of torque, consider a lever that is 6 feet long. An effort of 10 pounds is sufficient to lift a resistance of 20 pounds. Assuming that the lever remains rigid, the resistance will move a distance of 1½ feet when the effort moves a distance of 3 feet.

The work input for this lever is:

10 pounds x 3 feet = 30 *foot-pounds*.

The work output is:

20 pounds x 1½ feet = 30 *foot-pounds*.

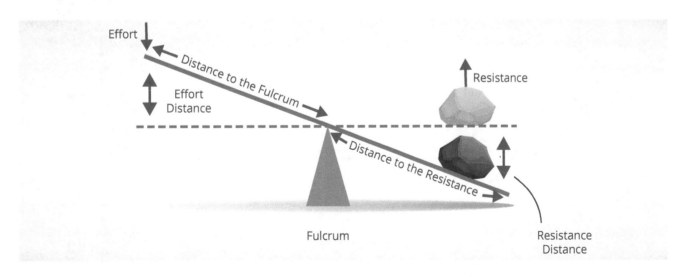

Effort

Distance to the Fulcrum

Effort Distance

Resistance

Distance to the Resistance

Fulcrum

Resistance Distance

This lever is an "ideal" lever in the sense that we have decided that it does not bend, nor is energy (work) lost to friction. Its efficiency, therefore, is 100 percent. We can show that the efficiency is 100 percent by calculating the AMA and the IMA and using either of the formulas:

$$\% \text{ efficiency} = \frac{\text{AMA}}{\text{IMA}} \times 100\%$$

or

$$\% \text{ efficiency} = \frac{\text{work output}}{\text{work input}} \times 100\%$$

The counterclockwise torque of this lever is:

> 20 pounds x 2 feet = 40 *foot-pounds*.

The clockwise torque is:

> 10 pounds x 4 feet = 40 *foot-pounds*.

When the clockwise and counterclockwise torques are equal, the lever is not spinning on its fulcrum; in other words, the lever is acting like a lever.

 Write true or false.

2.4 _____ Torque is the product of force and the distance through which force moves.

2.5 _____ Input work divided by output work equals the efficiency of a lever.

2.6 _____ An equal-arm balance is almost perfectly efficient.

2.7 _____ The less contact the fulcrum has with the lever, the less energy is lost to friction.

2.8 _____ Efficiency of a lever is not influenced by the skill of the user.

Complete this activity.

2.9 What force is required to balance the lever?

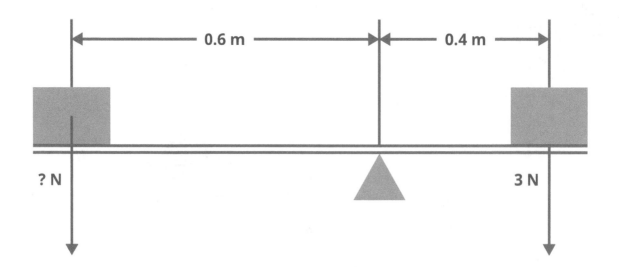

CLASSES OF LEVERS

Levers are classified according to the location of the fulcrum and the direction of the torques. The three classes have different uses, advantages, and disadvantages.

First-class. When the fulcrum, the point of balance, is located between the effort force and the resistance force, the lever is a first-class lever. The mechanical advantage increases as the fulcrum is moved closer to the resistance.

Seesaws are examples of first-class levers.

Second-class. A second-class lever finds the resistance between the fulcrum and the effort force. The mechanical advantage is always more than one and increases as the resistance approaches the fulcrum.

A wheelbarrow is an example of a second-class lever.

Third-class. When the effort force is between the resistance and the fulcrum, the lever is third-class. The mechanical advantage is always less than one, but speed is gained.

The human forearm is an example of a third-class lever. The elbow is the fulcrum, the resistance is in the hand, and the effort force is provided by the muscle attached to the forearm.

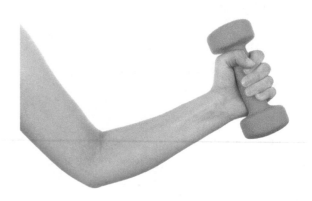

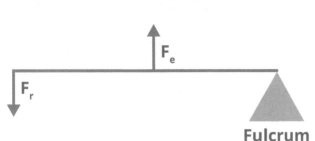

Fulcrum

Write true or false.

2.10 _____ A second-class lever places the resistance between the fulcrum and the effort force.

2.11 _____ A laboratory balance is a second-class lever.

2.12 _____ A third-class lever provides less mechanical advantage but more speed.

Complete these activities. State the class of lever for each picture.

2.13 The crowbar is a _____ -class lever.

2.14   This bottle opener is a _____ -class lever.

2.15   The baseball bat is a _____ -class lever.

2.16   A pair of pliers is a double _____ -class lever.

2.17   A pair of ice tongs is a double

_____ -class lever.

 **Review the material in this section in preparation for the Self Test.** The Self Test will check your mastery of this particular section. The items missed on this Self Test will indicate specific areas where restudy is needed for mastery.

SELF TEST 2

Write true or false (each answer, 1 point).

2.01 _____ A third-class lever increases the distance a load can be moved.

2.02 _____ Friction is not related to the efficiency of a machine.

2.03 _____ Actual mechanical advantage and ideal mechanical advantage are not always equal.

2.04 _____ Work output can never be greater than work input.

2.05 _____ Friction between our feet and the surface we walk on is desirable.

Match these items (each answer, 2 points).

2.06 _____ torque

2.07 _____ equal-arm balance

2.08 _____ efficiency of a lever

2.09 _____ streamlined shape

2.010 _____ fluid

a. almost perfectly efficient

b. either a gas or a liquid

c. direction the lever would spin if allowed to do so

d. second-class lever

e. output divided by input

f. reduces friction of an airplane

Write the letter for the correct answer (each answer, 2 points).

2.011 A bottle opener is an example of a _____ .
a. first-class lever   b. second-class lever c. third-class lever

2.012 A laboratory balance is an example of a _____ .
a. first-class lever   b. second-class lever c. third-class lever

2.013 A car wheel is an example of _____ .
a. sliding friction   b. rolling friction   c. fluid friction

2.014 A human forearm is an example of a _____ .
a. first-class lever   b. second-class lever c. third-class lever

2.015 A farmer dragging rocks from a field is an example of _____ .
a. sliding friction   b. rolling friction   c. fluid friction

Complete these calculations (each answer, 5 points).

2.016 A box weighing eight newtons requires a force of two newtons to push it along the floor.
What is the coefficient of friction between the box and the floor?

2.017 A lever is four meters long. A load of 1,200 newtons is placed one meter from the fulcrum.

a. What force will balance the 3-meter arm?

b. Friction requires an additional effort of 50 N.
The force needed to balance the 3-meter arm is now _____ .

SCIENCE 808

LIFEPAC TEST

NAME _____

DATE _____

SCORE _____

$$\frac{36}{45}$$

SCIENCE 808: LIFEPAC TEST

Write true or false (each answer, 1 point).

1. _____ Friction is the force that opposes motion.

2. _____ The inclined plane loses efficiency to sliding friction or rolling friction.

3. _____ Friction can be reduced by using a material that offers little resistance to another surface.

4. _____ Correct shape will reduce fluid friction.

5. _____ A pair of tweezers is an example of a third-class lever.

6. _____ The screw has a very low mechanical advantage.

7. _____ A nail is an example of a double inclined plane.

8. _____ A first-class lever is an almost perfectly efficient machine.

9. _____ The mechanical advantage of the wedge is decreased as it gets thinner.

10. _____ A single fixed pulley changes only the direction of the effort force.

Write the letter of the correct choice (each answer, 2 points).

11. Of two possible routes to the top of a hill, the steep slope requires _____ .
    a. a small force over a short distance   b. a small force over a long distance
    c. a large force over a short distance   d. a large force over a long distance

12. The incline of new federal highways may be as much as _____ percent.
    a. 3   b. 4   c. 8   d. 12

13. An example of a second-class lever is the _____ .
    a. bottle opener   b. laboratory balance
    c. seesaw   d. human forearm

14. An undesirable effect of friction is _____ .
    a. shoe on pavement   b. wheel on axle
    c. drive belt on pulley   d. tire on road

15. A wheel and axle system with the highest mechanical advantage has _____ .
    a. a small wheel and a small axle   b. a large wheel and a small axle
    c. a small wheel and a large axle   d. a large wheel and a large axle

Complete these calculations (each answer, 5 points).

16. Use the information given on the diagram to complete the calculations.

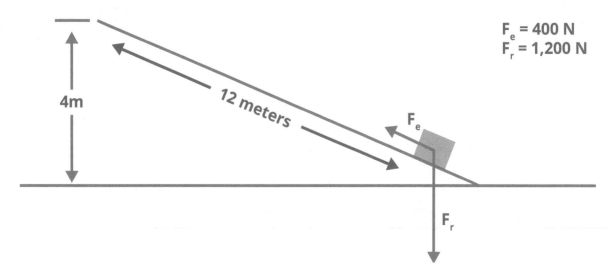

a. Calculate the IMA.

b. Calculate the AMA.

c. Calculate the efficiency in percent.

17. State which wedge will have a higher IMA. _____

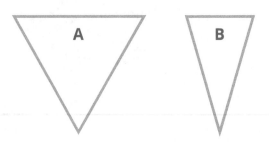

18. A box weighing 20 newtons requires a force of 8 newtons to push it along the floor. Calculate the coefficient of friction.

c. What is the IMA of the lever?

d. Based on part b, what is the AMA of the lever?

e. What is the efficiency of the lever?

SCORE _____   TEACHER _____ _____

initials   date

3. WHEEL AND AXLE, PULLEYS, AND GEARS

The invention of the **wheel** was a major step in the histories of mankind and of the machine. The Sumerians used the wheel as early as 3500 B.C. Their chariots were wooden and have since decomposed. The evidence of wooden-wheeled chariots exists today in pictures and molds. Evidence exists that by 2000 B.C. use of the wheel and **axle** had spread from China to the British Isles.

To make a wheel, people first had to learn to draw and cut an accurate circle. That step, in itself, was a major one. The wheel is generally viewed as a means of transportation, but it also was used horizontally as a potter's wheel. This application, too, was a major step forward.

The pulley came a little later in history, in the Middle East, as an outgrowth of the wheel and axle. Gears are one of the oldest methods of transmitting motion.

SECTION OBJECTIVES

Review these objectives. When you have completed this section, you should be able to:

7. List the uses of the wheel and axle, pulley, and gears.
8. Calculate the mechanical advantage of the wheel and axle and pulleys.

VOCABULARY

Study these words to enhance your learning success in this section.

axle (ak' sul). The shaft on which a wheel turns.

axis (ak' sis). An imaginary or real line that passes through an object, about which the object turns.

block and tackle (blok and tak' ul). A system of pulleys designed to lift a large weight with a small effort force.

gear (gir). A wheel with teeth that fit into the teeth of another wheel of the same kind to transmit motion.

pulley (pul' ē). A wheel having a grooved rim in which a rope can run to change direction of effort, or with a set of these wheels to increase the effort force.

wheel (hwēl). A round frame turning on a shaft in its center.

Try this investigation.

These supplies are needed:

- pencil sharpener (wall-mounted)
- book
- 2½ meters of string

Follow these directions and complete the sentence. Put a check in the box when each step is completed.

☐ 1. Remove the cover of the pencil sharpener.

☐ 2. Tie one end of the string around the book.

☐ 3. Tie the other end of the string around the axle of the pencil sharpener as shown in the drawing.

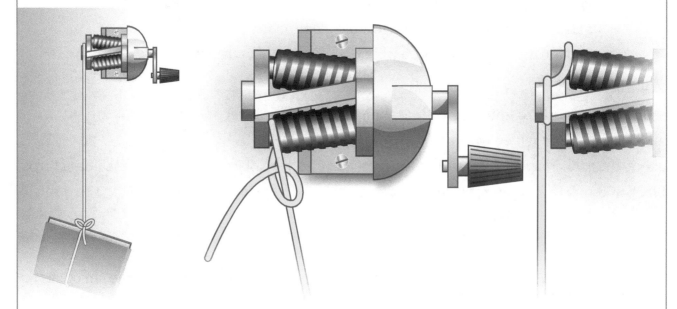

☐ 4. Turn the handle of the sharpener and raise the book to the level of the sharpener.

☐ 5. Untie the book and lift it the same distance by hand.

3.1 Using the wheel and axle (pencil sharpener) to raise the book required less _____ .

Wheel and Axle Experiment

WHEEL AND AXLE

A **wheel** and **axle** is a device that increases an effort force. The wheel and axle have the same **axis**.

Types. The idea of the wheel and axle is sometimes expressed as an axle with a crank, or lever, instead of a wheel. The effort force moves through a larger circle than does the resistance force. The wheel is attached to an axle or drum that has the same axis.

Mechanical advantages. The ideal mechanical advantage is found by dividing the circumference of the wheel (the effort distance) by the circumference of the axle (the resistance distance).The IMA can be increased by increasing the radius of the wheel and/or decreasing the radius of the axle. The same quotient is arrived at by dividing the wheel radius by the axle radius.

The actual mechanical advantage for the wheel and axle, as for the lever, is the resistance force divided by the effort force.

The efficiency, as in other machines, is found by dividing the AMA by the IMA.

Uses. The steering wheel of a car is an example of a wheel and axle. A small turn of the steering wheel turns the steering column of the heavy car. A water wheel is also a wheel and axle. Before steam power, the water wheel ground grain, sawed lumber, and powered machines by transforming the energy of falling water into mechanical energy. A door handle is a lever that turns the small axle, or shaft. A small force moves through a large distance in order to make the larger resistance force move.

Wheels are a part of our transportation system. They are found on everything from bicycles to eighteen-wheel trucks. When the axle turns the wheel, force is decreased; but distance is increased.

Write true or false.

3.2 _____ When using the wheel and axle, the effort force moves through a greater distance than the resistance force.

3.3 _____ A wheel and its axle have the same axis.

3.4 _____ The efficiency of the wheel can be found by dividing the IMA by the AMA.

Complete these activities.

3.5 A wheel with a radius of 25 centimeters has an axle with a radius of 5 centimeters. The IMA of this wheel is _____ .

3.6 The IMA of a wheel and axle could be increased by increasing the size of the

a. _____ and/or b. _____ the size of the axle.

PULLEYS

Before 200 B.C., Archimedes designed systems of **pulleys** to lift large weights. The original pulley was probably a rope passing over a roller, which might have developed from using a rope over a tree branch to lift weights.

Types. A single pulley, fixed in position, simply changes the *direction* of force.

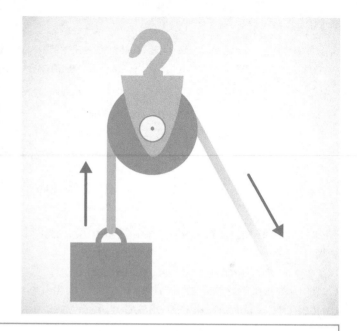

 Try this investigation; ask a classmate to help.

These supplies are needed:

- book
- string (1 meter long)
- sturdy coat hanger
- wire cutters
- spool

Follow these directions and complete the sentence. Put a check in the box when each step is completed.

- ☐ 1. Using the wire cutters, cut the long, straight wire from the coat hanger.
- ☐ 2. Bend it like the letter "L".
- ☐ 3. Slip the spool onto short leg of the "L".
- ☐ 4. Bend the end of the wire so the spool cannot slip off.
- ☐ 5. Tie the string around the book.
- ☐ 6. Pick up the book by the string.
- ☐ 7. Now ask your classmate to hold the "L".
  - ☐ 8. Pass the string over the spool.
  - ☐ 9. Pull the string to move the book.

  3.7   A single fixed pulley simply changes the _____ of the effort.

Pulley Experiment

A single movable pulley multiples the effort. The IMA of a single movable pulley is 2; that is, the effort force (F_e) of this system is half the resistance force (F_r), but the effort distance (d_e) is twice the resistance distance (d_r).

In a pulley system a 5 newton weight is to be lifted 2 meters. The rope is pulled 10 meters. The IMA is then 10 meters divided by 2 meters.

$$IMA = \frac{10 \text{ m}}{2 \text{ m}} = 5$$

In the same pulley system the 5 newton weight requires an effort force of 2 newtons. The AMA is found by dividing 5 newtons by 2 newtons.

$$AMA = \frac{5 \text{ N}}{2 \text{ N}} = 2.5$$

Mechanics often use a **block and tackle** to remove the engine from a car. A block and tackle is a system of pulleys used to lift heavy weights with a small effort force. This block and tackle multiplies the effort force five times (the IMA is 5). More pulleys would increase the IMA even more.

Mechanical advantage. The ideal mechanical advantage of a pulley can be found by counting the number of strands of rope that support the resistance. The IMA can be found also by dividing the effort distance by the resistance distance.

The AMA is found by dividing the resistance force by the effort force. The loss of effort to friction is greater with a system of pulleys than with a lever.

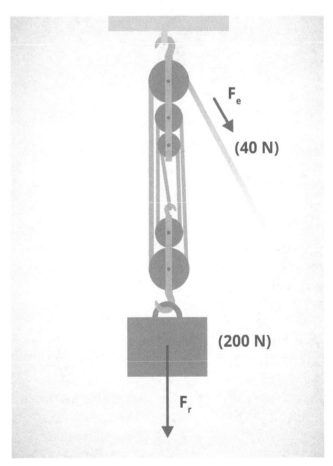

F_e

(40 N)

(200 N)

F_r

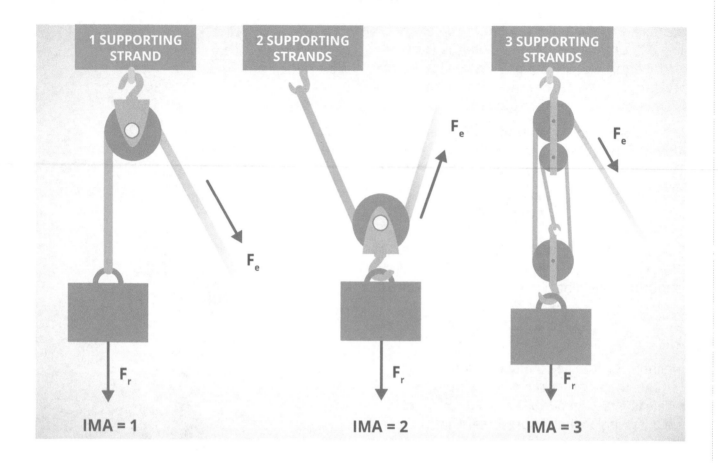

| 1 SUPPORTING STRAND | 2 SUPPORTING STRANDS | 3 SUPPORTING STRANDS |

F_e

F_r

IMA = 1

F_e

F_r

IMA = 2

F_e

F_r

IMA = 3

Uses. Pulleys transfer power from electric motors to machines. A v-belt passes around the drive pulley and the driven pulley. The speed of the driven pulley can be changed by changing the size of the pulley.

Generally, pulleys change the direction of the force or increase the effort force. The single pulley mounted over a well has been used since ancient times to haul water to the surface. The bucket and water is the resistance and the effort is provided by the person pulling on the rope. The single pulley is so common in daily life that we seldom think about it. Everything from raising the flag, to pulling your bike or canoe up to the ceiling in the garage to store it out of the way are ways that single pulleys are used.

| Single pulley and bucket over a water well

Match these items.

3.8	_____ single fixed pulley	a.	system of pulleys
3.9	_____ single movable pulley	b.	changes direction of effort
3.10	_____ block and tackle	c.	decreases distance
		d.	effort is one-half of the resistance

Complete these sentences.

3.11 A block and tackle system has four supporting strands so its IMA is _____ .

3.12 The pulley has a greater effort loss to _____ than does the lever.

Complete this activity.

3.13 A woman must lift a 40 newton box a height of 4 meters. She is using a single movable pulley. The amount of effort needed to raise the box is _____ newtons.

GEARS

The use of **gears** (wheels with teeth) is an easy method of transferring motion through short distances. It is one of the oldest methods of transmitting motion.

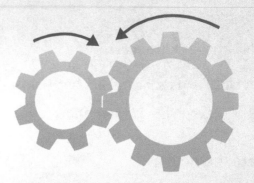

**Gears the same size
change the direction of motion**

**Gears of different size
change speed and direction**

 Try this observation.

The following item is needed:

■ hand eggbeater

Follow these directions and answer the question. Put a check in the box when each step is completed.

☐ 1. Place the knob of the handle at the bottom of its turning circle.

☐ 2. Turn the handle very slowly in one complete circle.

☐ 3. Count the number of times the blades go around as the handle is turned once.

3.14 How many times did the blades go around compared to one turn of the handle? _____

Gears Experiment

Types. Gears of the same size simply transfer motion. If the gears are of different sizes, the larger one turns more slowly; it turns with greater force, and through a smaller distance than the gear with the smaller radius.

Gear systems may transfer motion, speed it up, or slow it down. Gears also change direction.

Uses. Clocks have many gears. Early clocks had wooden gears. Today watches have brass and steel gears.

Factories use systems of belts and gears to drive machinery from a central energy system or motor. Workshop tools—drills, saws, lathes, and routers—use gears.

Gears of an automobile transmission transfer power from the engine to the rear wheels by way of the driveshaft.

All forms of transportation from bicycles to airplanes use gears. They transfer energy and speed machines up or slow them down.

Kitchen appliances, such as mixers and can openers, use gears to transfer the power of a fast-spinning electric motor to the job for which the appliance was designed.

 Complete these activities.

3.15 A large gear has 57 teeth and a smaller one has 19 teeth. Divide the number of teeth on the large gear by the number on the smaller gear to find the number of times the small gear will go around when the large gear goes around once.

The small gear will turn _____ times when the larger gear turns once.

3.16 List the steps needed to calculate the number of times a bicycle wheel would turn when the pedals go around once.

a. _____

_____

b. _____

_____

Complete these sentences.

3.17 Gears of the same size transfer _____ .

3.18 Gears of different sizes change a. _____ and b. _____ .

Underline the correct answer.

3.19   Gear B will turn in a (clockwise, counterclockwise) direction.

3.20   Gear C will turn in a (clockwise, counterclockwise) direction.

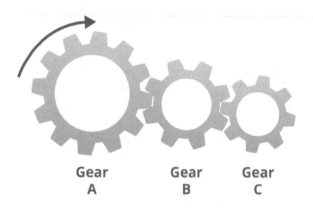

Gear
A

Gear
B

Gear
C

TEACHER CHECK _____ _____

initials   date

 Review the material in this section to prepare for the Self Test. This Self Test will check your mastery of this particular section as well as your knowledge of all previous sections.

SELF TEST 3

Write true or false (each answer, 1 point).

3.01 _____ A wheel and axle multiplies the effort force and the distance through which the effort force moves.

3.02 _____ Lubrication can decrease friction.

3.03 _____ A single movable pulley requires an effort that is one-half the resistance.

3.04 _____ Each supporting strand of a block and tackle increases the effort force by one-half.

3.05 _____ A pair of scissors is an example of a double first-class lever.

3.06 _____ A single fixed pulley changes the effort force in direction.

3.07 _____ The IMA of the wheel can be increased by increasing the size of the wheel.

3.08 _____ The IMA of the wheel can be increased by decreasing the size of the axle.

Complete these sentences (each answer, 3 points).

3.09 The IMA of a pulley can be found by counting the strands supporting the _____ .

3.010 One of the oldest methods of transmitting motion is the use of _____ .

3.011 A streamlined shape can lessen _____ .

3.012 AMA is found by dividing resistance force by _____ .

3.013 The IMA of the wheel and axle can be found by dividing the radius of the wheel by the radius of the _____ .

Complete these calculations (each answer, 5 points).

3.014 A wheel with a radius of 18 centimeters has an axle with a radius of 3 centimeters. Calculate IMA of this system.

3.015 A man is using a combination of one fixed pulley and one movable pulley to lift a box. Find how much his effort force is multiplied.

3.016 A large gear has 39 teeth and a small one has 13 teeth. Calculate how many times the small gear will turn when the large gear turns 4½ times.

3.017 In a pulley system a 5 newton weight is to be lifted 2 meters. The rope is pulled 10 meters. The effort force is two newtons.

    a. Calculate the IMA of this system.

    b. Calculate the AMA of this system.

    c. Calculate the efficiency of this system in percent.

Complete this item (this answer, 5 points).

3.018 Explain why the efficiency of a machine is always less than 100 percent.

_____

_____

_____

_____

$\dfrac{46}{58}$

SCORE _____ TEACHER _____ _____

                                                                                                 initials   date

4. INCLINED PLANE, WEDGE, AND SCREW

Many forms of the **inclined plane** exist and are used every day. Basically, a **wedge** is a double inclined plane, and a **screw** is an inclined plane wrapped around a cylinder. From the six basic machines all machines and tools are made.

When Jesus worked in Nazareth with His father Joseph, the carpenter tools they used were made from these simple machines. Carpenter tools today are still similar to those Jesus used. Machines make work easier for us, but work remains a necessity.

Even as Jesus worked with His hands and His mind, we are expected to work. Luke 10:7 reminds us that "...the laborer is worthy of his hire...." Knowledge and machines have taken some of the physical strain from work, but since Adam and Eve humans have needed to work. In Genesis 3:19 the Bible tell us, "In the sweat of thy face shalt thou eat bread...."

SECTION OBJECTIVES

Review these objectives. When you have completed this section, you should be able to:

9. Identify the uses of the inclined plane, wedge, and screw.

10. Calculate the mechanical advantage of the inclined plane, wedge, and screw.

VOCABULARY

Study these words to enhance your learning success in this section.

external (ek stėr' nul). On the outside.

inclined plane (in klīnd' plān). A ramp or a slope.

internal (in tėr' nul). On the inside.

screw (skrü). An inclined plane wrapped around a cylinder.

wedge (wej). A double inclined plane.

INCLINED PLANE

Every time you climb a hill you are climbing an **inclined plane**. Mountain climbers sometimes go up the steep slope of a mountain for its challenge and excitement. Other times they seek a more gentle slope. A steep slope demands more force over a short distance; the gentle slope requires less force over a long distance.

Uses. The inclined plane is a simple machine. It multiples effort force and is used to raise heavy objects. The slope is the major reason an inclined plane is a useful machine.

Ramps provided for wheelchairs are inclined planes. They must have a slope gentle enough to permit the person in the chair to get up easily and down safely. When a new federal highway is built, no slope can exceed 8 percent; that is, over a 100 meter distance the vertical rise cannot be more than 8 meters.

Mechanical advantage. The ideal mechanical advantage is the length (the effort distance) of the ramp divided by its vertical height (the resistance distance). The IMA is always greater than one.

The actual mechanical advantage is the resistance force divided by the effort force. Friction is a major problem in the use of the inclined plane.

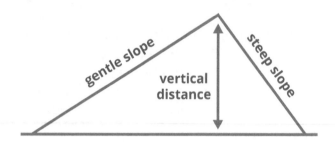

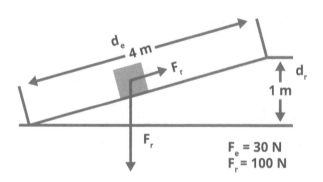

From this illustration we can calculate the AMA, IMA, and efficiency.

$$AMA = \frac{F_r}{F_e} = \frac{100\ N}{30\ N} = 3.\overline{3}$$

$$IMA = \frac{d_e}{d_r} = \frac{4\ m}{1\ m} = 4$$

$$\%\ efficiency = \frac{AMA}{IMA} = \frac{3.\overline{3}}{4} = 83.3\%$$

To increase the mechanical advantage, increase the length of the ramp.

Try this investigation.

These supplies are needed:

- rubber band (medium size)
- match box full of pebbles
- two rulers of different lengths
- three or four books

Follow these directions and complete the sentences. Put a check in the box when each step is completed.

☐ 1. Prop rulers of different lengths as inclined planes on the pile of books.

☐ 2. Attach the rubber band to the match box.

☐ 3. Pull the box up the side of the books without using the rulers and notice how far the rubber band is stretched.

☐ 4. Pull the box up the shorter of the two rulers and notice how far the rubber band is stretched.

☐ 5. Pull the box up the longer of the two rulers and again notice how far the rubber band is stretched.

4.1 The rubber band stretched the most when it was pulled up the

_____ .

4.2 The longer the inclined plane, the less the _____ required.

Inclined Plane Experiment

 Complete these sentences.

4.3 An inclined plane reduces the _____ needed to move a load vertically.

4.4 A gentle slope takes a a. _____ force over a b. _____ distance.

4.5 A steep slope takes a a. _____ force over a b. _____ distance.

4.6 To increase IMA, increase the _____ of the ramp.

4.7 A major factor in the use of the inclined plane is _____ .

Complete these calculations.

4.8 Using the information given on the diagram, complete these calculations.

a. Calculate the AMA.

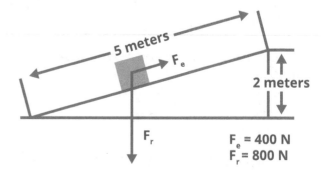

b. Calculate the IMA.

c. Calculate the efficiency in percent.

WEDGES

Wedges have been used throughout history. The person who invented the first knife was actually making a wedge. Abraham Lincoln split rails with another kind of wedge, the ax.

Types. A wedge is made of wood or metal with a thick edge at one end that slopes into a thin edge at the other end. As with the inclined plane, a longer wedge uses less effort force to split a log.

Uses. The knife and the ax are forms of wedges with a lever handle to increase the effort force. A chisel and a nail are wedges that are struck with a hammer. The wedge is used to split wood by being pounded into wood. The thinner the wedge, the easier the wood is to split.

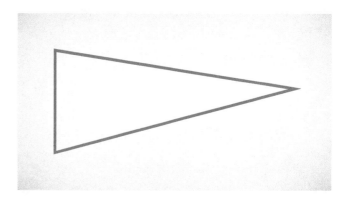

Mechanical advantage. The mechanical advantage is greater for thinner wedges. The efficiency is low because of the large amount of friction.

 Complete these statements.

4.9 The mechanical advantage of the wedge increases as it gets _____ .

4.10 The efficiency of the wedge is low because of _____ .

SCREW

The **screw** utilizes the mechanical advantage of the inclined plane when used as a fastener. Early clamps were made of wood and tightened with a wooden screw. Such wooden clamps are still used for some purposes, such as furniture repair.

Types. If you cut out a piece of paper in the shape of an inclined plane and wind it around your pencil, you will see the inclined plane turn into a screw. The inclined plane winds spirally around the solid cylinder. The ridge forming the inclined plane is the *thread*. A thread can also be located inside a cylinder.

Uses. This simple machine, the screw, has many applications. It can be used to fasten one object to another. It can be used as a nut and a bolt. The bolt has an **external** thread. The nut has an identical **internal** thread.

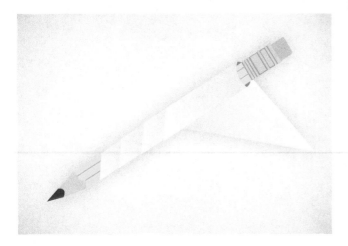

This same internal-external thread combination is the basis for the *jackscrew*. The internal screw is the base. The external screw is on a metal cylinder. A lever handle is at the top of the external screw. As the handle is rotated, the external screw moves up the threads of the internal screw. The weight on top of the jack is lifted. This machine has much friction but lifts large loads because the inclined plane of which it is made is very long.

Mechanical advantage. The ideal mechanical advantage of a screw is found by dividing the distance the effort moves in one full turn by the distance from one thread to the next. The input work of a screw is greater than the output work. The efficiency of the screw is very low; however, it is used because the small effort needed to turn the handle will lift enormous loads.

Write true or false.

4.11 _____ A screw is simply a form of a wedge.

4.12 _____ The screw has very low efficiency.

Complete this activity.

4.13 Make a list of ten places where some application of the screw is used.

_____   _____

_____   _____

_____   _____

_____   _____

_____   _____

TEACHER CHECK _____ _____
                          initials   date

Before you take this last Self Test, you may want to do one or more of these self checks.

1. _____ Read the objectives. See if you can do them.
2. _____ Restudy the material related to any objectives that you cannot do.
3. _____ Use the **SQ3R** study procedure to review the material:
   a. **S**can the sections.
   b. **Q**uestion yourself.
   c. **R**ead to answer your questions.
   d. **R**ecite the answers to yourself.
   e. **R**eview areas you did not understand.
4. _____ Review all vocabulary, activities, and Self Tests, writing a correct answer for every wrong answer.

SELF TEST 4

Match these items (each answer, 2 points).

Type of machine		Example	
4.01	_____ gear	a.	seesaw
4.02	_____ block and tackle	b.	bottle opener
4.03	_____ first-class lever	c.	oil
4.04	_____ inclined plane	d.	nail
4.05	_____ wheel and axle	e.	bolt and nut
4.06	_____ second-class lever	f.	pencil sharpener
4.07	_____ wedge	g.	clock
4.08	_____ screw	h.	ramp
4.09	_____ third-class lever	i.	forearm
4.010	_____ single fixed pulley	j.	used to lift an engine
		k.	can only change the direction of a force

Complete these sentences (each answer, 3 points).

4.011 Machines are made less efficient by _____ .

4.012 Each supporting strand of a block and tackle increases the effort force by _____ .

4.013 A single fixed pulley changes the direction of the _____ .

4.014 Gears of different sizes change speed and _____ .

4.015 The mechanical advantage of the inclined plane can be increased by increasing the ramp's

_____ .

4.016 Friction can be reduced by using oil or grease, which are _____ .

4.017 A wedge has a higher IMA as it gets _____ .

Complete these calculations (each answer, 3 points).

4.018 A box weighing 24 newtons requires a force of 16 newtons to drag it.
What is the coefficient of friction?

4.019 A lever 10 meters long has a load of 9,000 newtons placed 4 meters from the fulcrum.
A force of 7,500 newtons is placed on the 6 meter arm.

a. Calculate the IMA.

b. Calculate the AMA.

c. Calculate the efficiency (in percent).

4.020 A wheel has a radius of 9 centimeters and an axle radius of 3 centimeters.
Calculate the IMA of the system.

4.021 A large gear has 24 teeth and a smaller gear has 8 teeth.
How many times will the smaller gear turn as the large gear turns once?

4.022 A four-strand pulley system is used to lift a 120 newton load.
Calculate the effort force needed.

SCORE _____ TEACHER _____ _____
initials   date

Before taking the LIFEPAC Test, you may want to do one or more of these self checks.

1. _____ Read the objectives. See if you can do them.
2. _____ Restudy the material related to any objectives that you cannot do.
3. _____ Use the **SQ3R** study procedure to review the material.
4. _____ Review activities, Self Tests, and LIFEPAC vocabulary words.
5. _____ Restudy areas of weakness indicated by the last Self Test.